Anim N

Written by Jillian Powell

Contents

◌ Collins

War work

Animals did important work in both world wars. They carried heavy loads.

World War I was between 1914 and 1918, and World War II was between 1939 and 1945.

They carried messages that saved lives. They sniffed out bombs and mines.

3

Horses and mules

Horses and mules carried men and weapons to battle.

AT THE FRONT!

Every fit Briton should join our brave men at the Front.

ENLIST NOW.

OUR DUMB FRIENDS' LEAGUE
(A Society for the Encouragement of Kindness to Animals)
President : THE RIGHT HON. THE EARL OF LONSDALE
BLUE CROSS FUND
President : LADY SMITH-DORRIEN

Please help the Horses

At the Front and at Home

Nationality not considered

All Suffering Horses Relieved

DONATIONS URGENTLY NEEDED
Also HORSE CLOTHING and all VETERINARY REQUISITES

London, S.W.

posters from the war

More than eight million horses were killed in World War I.

Elephants

Elephants pulled heavy loads too.

They helped to build bridges and clear roads. They could cross rivers and get into jungles to rescue people trapped by war.

Pigeons

Pigeons carried important messages home when radio could not be used.

The pigeon carried a tiny metal container
on its leg.
The message was rolled up inside it.

Dogs

Dogs carried messages too, in containers on their collars. They also sniffed out mines or wounded men.

10

"Paradogs" jumped from planes with parachute troops. As soon as they landed, they used their noses and ears to warn soldiers if there was danger from mines or enemy troops.

Dogs were also kept as mascots to bring comfort and good luck.

11

Brave animals

Millions of animals were very brave during the wars.

This memorial in London remembers the bravery of animals in wartime.

Some won medals for their work, but many more were killed.

13

How animals helped in war

carrying heavy loads

sniffing out mines

clearing roads

carrying messages

parachuting to help soldiers

Index

Ideas for reading

Written by Gillian Howell
Primary Literacy Consultant

Learning objectives: *(reading objectives correspond with Blue band; all other objectives correspond with Diamond band)* use phonics to read unknown words; understand underlying themes, causes and points of view; appraise a text quickly, deciding on its value, quality or usefulness; use the techniques of dialogic talk to explore ideas, topics or issues; use varied structures to shape and organise text coherently

Curriculum links: History: What was it like to live here in the past?; Citizenship: Animals and us

High frequency words: did, in, they, was, that, out, and, to, more, than, eight, were, too, could, people, by, home, when, not, be, a, on, its, up, it, dogs, too, their, or, from, with, as, if, there, good, of, very, the, this, some, but, many

Interest words: mules, elephants, pigeons, weapons, rescue, jungles, danger, monument

Resources: paper, pens, pencils, whiteboard

Word count: 212

Getting started

- Read the title together and look at the front cover, discussing what first impression it gives them. Turn to the back cover and ask them to read the blurb.

- Encourage the children to suggest what sort of work animals did in the world wars and make notes on a whiteboard. Encourage them to give reasons for their opinions.

- Read the contents page together. Ask the children if they know what a mule is. If they have difficulty with the word, prompt them to pronounce the *u* as the letter name. Ask the children if there are any particular chapters they might want to read first, or should they start at the beginning and read in sequence?

Reading and responding

- Ask the children to read the text quietly. Remind them to use their phonic knowledge to work out new words and break longer words into syllables.

- Ask the children, as they read, to identify and note three key activities of animals in the wars and why they were useful.